Elon Musk

Elon Musk's greatest lessons for success in business, life, and entrepreneurship

Table of Contents

Introduction

Thank you for taking the time to pick up this book about Elon Musk!

This book aims to serve as somewhat of a biography-to-date of the incredible entrepreneur that is Elon Musk. Elon is well known for his ventures with Tesla Motors, and also with SpaceX, but he has been involved in many other businesses as you will soon find out.

In the following chapters, you will learn about Elon's childhood, his time in college, his early experiences with business, the different companies he has launched or invested in, and much more!

Hopefully this book can inspire you through the telling of Elon Musk's story, as well as provide you with some insight as to what is next for the legendary entrepreneur.

Once again, thanks for choosing this book! I hope you find it to be both interesting and insightful!

Chapter 1: About Elon Musk

Elon Reeve Musk was born in South Africa on 28th June, in the year 1971. He spent most of his childhood and adolescent years in South Africa. Elon's parents are Maye and Errol Musk.

His father, Errol Musk, who was an engineer, primarily raised Elon. Elon had a keen mind, was fascinated by computers from an early age, and started programming during his early teenage years.

Elon's parents divorced in the year 1980, and he lived with his father for most of the time afterwards. It was during this period that he developed a fascination for computing by using Commodore VIC-20. He learned computer programming on his own, and he made use of this for coding a video game. At the tender age of 12, Musk had written the code for Balstar, a video game, while he was still in South Africa. He sold this video game for a profit of $500. The code that Musk had written was never really converted into an official game. However, in the year 1984, the source code of this video game was published by PC and Office Technology, a trade publication.

Musk has two siblings, a younger brother Kimbal and his sister Tosca. When their parents separated they stayed primarily with their father. They traveled quite a lot with their father growing up. Kimbal used to help in navigation and guiding; he was quite an energetic child. Elon, on the other hand, was an introvert and a deep thinker. For instance, if they were all invited over to a party, everyone would be busy socializing or drinking or engaging in other fun activities, while Elon would wander off in search of the person's library and would go through their books. This is how Elon would have fun and he never really was a party person.

The way Elon thought and the ideas he would come up with would always surprise Errol Musk, and these things made him realize that his son was indeed different from an average kid his age.

The Musk family is quite fascinating. Elon's grandmother was the first chiropractor in Canada. His grandparents were also the first ones to cover the distance between South Africa and Australia in a single-engine plane. Elon's father was quite dynamic. He was a pilot, sailor, and an engineer as well, and he raised his children in the peaceful suburbs of Pretoria.

At present, Elon's siblings are doing quite well for themselves. Tosca is a producer as well as a director. Kimbal Musk owns a couple of chains of restaurants and also spearheads an NPO called The Kitchen Community that helps in growing vegetables in the US.

Elon was bullied a lot while growing up. It was perhaps his introverted nature that caused all the other children at his school to bully him. After the worst instance of bullying he experienced, Musk had to be hospitalized because he had blacked out after he was thrown down a flight of stairs. Fortunately, he overcame all the unpleasant experiences of his childhood and didn't let this deter him from being himself. He was smarter than the other kids, and he made sure that he excelled in his studies. His inclination towards physics, space engineering, and coding helped in shaping his future.

He was quite independent while growing up and he proved this when he decided to migrate to Canada without his parent's support. His eventual move to the United States wasn't a smooth one. He had migrated to Canada and attained a Canadian citizenship before he moved to Montreal. He started out by working odd jobs that paid meager wages. He studied in Ontario for two years before relocating to the USA. In the year 1992, he got a scholarship to study at The University of Pennsylvania. He then went on to obtain his Bachelor's degree in physics and then another one in Economics from Wharton School. His real journey, however, started when he dropped out of Stanford to pursue his dream of starting his own company.

In the year 1995, Musk enrolled himself in a Ph.D. program in applied physics at the renowned Stanford University, California. However, he dropped out of this course shortly later, realizing that it wasn't the path he should be taking. Instead, Elon sought to start his own company. This company was Zip2, and he went on to sell it to Compaq for a little over $300-million in the year 1999. Due to giving up equity to investors, the amount he received from this sale was $22 million, and he made use of this by funding his next startup, X.com.

X.com was an online banking site, and it was later rechristened as PayPal! EBay acquired this company for $1.5-billion in the year 2002 and Musk received stock in this company valued at $165-million. He also became an American citizen in that same year. Fresh from the sale of PayPal, Musk decided to pursue his interest in space engineering. He started his own company, SpaceX, which developed its own rockets and various other things.

The company managed to launch its first commercial spacecraft in the year 2009 and then again in 2012. While he was thinking about expanding into the field of space engineering, something on Earth caught his eye as well. He was interested in the field of transportation also. In 2004, he joined the Board of Tesla Motors as the Chairman. He played a significant role in designing the cars that Tesla was manufacturing. After the financial crisis of 2008, Musk took over the position of CEO at Tesla, and he still holds this position today.

Overview of his journey

After Elon dropped out of Stanford, he and his brother had borrowed a sum of $28,000 from their father and decided to launch their own software company. They named it as Zip2, and it was started in the year 1995. The Internet was still in its infancy at this time, and it wasn't yet popular. Also, at this time newspapers and magazines were looking for ways in which they could make the most of the different media for increasing their readership. They wanted to be able to expand the reach of their newspapers. The Musk brothers decided to help the publishers of newspapers by developing city guides for them that could be published online. Soon after launching, their company received contracts from big players in this field, and their client list included the New York Times and the Chicago Tribune. They eventually managed to convince their board of directors to change their business plans for a merger with CitySearch.

Once Elon had sold his company, Zip2, he cofounded another one named X.com. This company was later merged with Confinity, and then they renamed the entire company PayPal. The merged company's main focus was on the money transfer service that PayPal offered. Their viral marketing campaigns helped in promoting the growth of PayPal, and their customer base started growing rapidly. In the year 2000, Musk was overthrown from the position he held as the CEO of the company (though he was still a part of the board of directors). This move was due to certain disagreements with others over his idea of moving the Unix-based infrastructure of PayPal to Microsoft Windows.

All these things happened whilst Musk had gone on his first vacation in a long time. He was still on the flight that was en route to Australia when the Board fired him as the CEO and made the decision of appointing Peter Thiel in his place. PayPal was sold to eBay shortly after in late 2002, and Elon received a handsome settlement. However, this wasn't the end of the journey for Musk. This was merely a stepping-stone for him, and he was yet to get started on his ambitious projects.

One of his major interests was space exploration, and in 2001 he started to realize this dream of his. He began to conceptualize a project that involved the maintaining of an experimental greenhouse that could survive on Mars. This greenhouse would be capable of sustaining food crops, and he named this experimental project 'Mars Oasis'. He had even traveled to Moscow for acquiring Inter-Continental Ballistic Missiles (also known as ICBMs) for transporting things in space. He met with a lot of leading companies. However, he was written off as a novice and wasn't given the assistance he required. This didn't deter Musk in his endeavor of realizing his dream of space exploration. He approached different companies in the following months, though the subsequent meetings proved to be futile.

The bids he received for his requirements were quite high, and Elon didn't want to take these offers. While this happened, he realized something. He had decided that he could start a company on his own that will help him in building the rockets he needed, but he could do so at an affordable price. He discovered that he could build a rocket that would cost about 3% of the estimated sales price of a rocket at that point in time. He managed to set up SpaceX from the proceeds of the sale of PayPal.

Within a span of seven years, SpaceX has managed to accomplish the designing of Falcon launch vehicles and the Dragon spacecraft. Both of them have been berthed at the ISS. SpaceX become the largest private producer of rocket motors in the whole world! At present Elon has been working on designing the first unmanned flight to Mars that would be a part of the Mars Colonial Transporter (known as MCT) spacecraft that is scheduled for departure to Mars in the year 2022. The first manned MCT Mars flight would soon follow suit in 2024 if everything goes well. Musk has always been curious about space exploration and travel and has stated in multiple interviews that he dreams of colonizing Mars!

In the year 2003, Tesla Motors was incorporated by Martin Eberhard and Marc Tarpenning, and they started this unit with their own funds. Both of these men had played a major role in the shaping of this company and its development in the early years. This company made use of the funds of the people who incorporated it until the Series-A round of funding. This funding took place in the year 2004, in the month of February and they received the necessary funds they needed primarily from Musk. This led to Musk becoming a part of Tesla as the chairman of its Board. However, Elon was never really involved in the daily operations of the business, but he did have an active role in the company, and he supervised the product design from the basic level for the Roadster project.

In the year 2008, the US economy came crashing down. This was when Musk took over as the CEO of Tesla Motors. Under his leadership, Tesla Motors created the Tesla Roadster in the year 2008, which is an electric sports car. The sales of this particular model were recorded at 2500 vehicles in 31 countries. In the year 2010, Tesla came out with its IPO. The second car manufacturing company to have launched an IPO is Tesla, after Ford. Even though Tesla wasn't profitable for ten years, it was listed on NASDAQ, and its stock was priced at $17 per share. Tesla managed to attract over $25-million in public investment.

The company has managed to develop different models of cars, including the 4-door S-Model Sedan, Model X, the electric powertrain system for Daimler for Mercedes B-class electric drive, Smart EV, Mercedes A-class, as well as for the Toyota RAV4 EV. Musk owns approximately 29 million shares in Tesla (that's 22% of the company stock) and takes home an annual salary of $1, just like Steve Jobs and Mark Zuckerberg. The rest of his compensation is paid to him in the form of bonuses based on performance and stock options.

Family Tree

Maye was Elon Musk's mother. She was a dietician, and she also dabbled in a little bit of modeling. She was an avid reader, just like Elon. At the age of 22, she married Errol Musk. Errol obtained her dietician degree from the University of Pretoria. After marriage, she conceived three children and started her counseling practice. Errol Musk was of British origin, and he was born in South Africa. He was an engineer. Elon has two siblings, Tosca and Kimbal. Tosca is a known actress and a producer as well. She is known for her movies like Simple Things and The heavy. Kimbal Musk was born on September 20, in the year 1972. Kimbal, like Elon has had several entrepreneurial ventures.

Elon Musk was first married to Justine Wilson. Musk met Justine while he was in Kingston, studying at Queen's University. They got married in the year 2000, and they had five children together. They divorced in the year 2008. Musk is now married to Tallulah Riley. Tallulah Riley is a British actress and is known for her performance in Pride and Prejudice and The boat that rocked.

Advisor to Donald Trump

Donald Trump, the current President, has named Musk as a part of his business advisory team for his administration term. Travis Kalanick and Indra Nooyi are also part of this team. Trump's administration aims to work closely with the private sector for improving the business environment and attract more firms for creating new job opportunities in the US.

Elon Musk- Timeline

- ➢ He was born on 28 June 1971 in South Africa.

- ➢ Wrote the code for Balstar at the age of 12 and sold it for $500.

- ➢ He graduated from Pretoria Boys High School with a distinction in science and computer studies in 1988.

- ➢ He attended college at the Queen's University in Ontario between 1989 and 1991. He then took a transfer to the University of Pennsylvania and completed a BS in Economics and BA (majoring in physics).

- ➢ Shifted to Silicon Valley in 1995 and enrolled in the Ph.D. program of applied physics at Stanford University, but dropped out immediately to start his company.

- ➢ In 1999 he sold Zip2 to Compaq for $307 million and formed X.com (renamed as PayPal in 2000).

- ➢ In 2002, July eBay acquired PayPal for $1.5 billion, and Musk received $165 million in stock.

- ➢ In 2002, he became a citizen of the United States of America and founded SpaceX.

- ➢ In 2006, he financed Tesla Motors.

- ➢ In 2007, SpaceX secured a $1.6 billion contract for transporting cargo to International Space Station (ISS).

- ➢ In 2008, he became the CEO at Tesla.

- In 2010, Tesla announced its IPO.

- In 2012, SpaceX became the first commercial vehicle for transporting cargo to the International Space Station.

- In 2012, June, Tesla began the delivery of the fully electric Model S.

- In 2013, August, Musk released the sketch and the concept of the Hyperloop.

Chapter 2: Elon's early life

Elon Musk moved from South Africa to Canada in the year 1988. He was 17 years old at the time and hoped that he could someday emigrate to the US from there. However, his move to Canada wasn't well thought out. Musk knew a great-uncle of his who happened to stay in Montreal. Musk simply hopped on a flight and to put it mildly "hoped for the best."

Upon landing in Montreal, Musk tried to contact his uncle by making use of a pay phone and the directory assistance service. He couldn't, however, locate his great uncle. Musk then called his mother, and she had bad news for him. Maye had written that uncle a letter before Musk had left from South Africa and she received a reply while Musk was in transit. The uncle had gone to Minnesota, and this meant Musk had nowhere to go. Carrying his bags, he headed towards a youth hostel. He spent a few days exploring Montreal, and while doing so, he was trying hard to come up with a plan that would work. His mother had relatives who were scattered all across Canada and Musk started reaching out to them. He purchased a countrywide bus pass for $100 that would allow him to hop on and off the buses as he pleased, and the town that he headed to was Saskatchewan. This was where his grandfather used to live.

He ended up in the town of Swift Current after a long journey of 1900 miles. This town had a population of fifteen thousand people. The minute Musk got off at the bus station, he phoned his second cousin from the bus station and went to his home. He spent the next year working a string of odd jobs around the country. He would tend to vegetables and shovel out the grain bins at his cousin's farm that was located in Waldeck, a very small town. He got to celebrate his 18th birthday at this place, and shared a cake with a family he had just met, as well as a bunch of strangers from around the neighborhood. After this,

Musk's next job was to cut logs with a chainsaw back in Vancouver.

Perhaps the hardest job that he took up came after his visit to the unemployment office. He inquired about the details of the job that would pay him the most. This gig turned out to be quite difficult, but it paid the most out of the lot. He would be paid $18 per hour for cleaning out the boiler room in a lumber mill. Musk would have to don a HAZMAT suit and then squeeze himself through a very small tunnel.

Once he was inside the tunnel, he would then have to shovel out sand, goop, and any other residue, that was still steaming hot through the same hole that he had entered the tunnel from. There was no escape route. Someone on the other end would need to keep shoving all that into a wheelbarrow. It would get so hot in the tunnel that he could die from the heat if he got stuck down there for more than 30 minutes. Musk was amongst the thirty people who had opted for this job. Three days into his work and only five people remained there. By the end of the week, it was just Elon and two other men who hadn't quit.

Whilst Musk was still making his way around Canada, his mom, brother, and sister were trying to figure out a way in which they could get there as well. When Musk was reunited with his brother Kimbal in Canada, their playful and headstrong natures blossomed. In 1989, Elon had enrolled himself at the Queen's University in Kingston, in the city of Ontario. Elon opted for this University over the University of Waterloo, since he felt that there were better-looking women at the former.

When Musk wasn't studying, he would read the newspaper with Kimbal, and they would start identifying "interesting" people with whom they would like to meet. Once this was done, they would take turns in cold-calling these people and asking them if they would be available to have lunch. The Musk brothers did harass a few people in their time. The list of those harassed includes the head of the marketing division of the Toronto Blue Jays, a business writer for the Globe and the Mail, and also a top executive of The Bank of Nova Scotia, Peter Nicholson. Nicholson remembers the calls the boys used to make, since he wasn't used to getting any requests without prior notice.

It took Nicholson about six months to clear his schedule up, and he was willing to have lunch with the kids who had called him. The Musk brothers traveled for about 3 hours for meeting Nicholson.

After their first meeting, Nicholson was left with quite a good impression of these siblings. The brothers were both polite and even presented themselves quite well. However, Elon and Kimbal do have opposite personalities. Kimbal is charismatic and personable whereas Elon is quite geeky and awkward to a certain extent. Nicholson was captivated with this duo, and he ended up offering Elon an internship for summer at the bank, and later on became his most trusted advisor.

Chapter 3: Elon's life in college

Musk enjoyed himself in college and was noted to be aspiring and determined. He worked on cultivating his intellectual abilities and looking for people who respected them. He participated in college activities like public speaking, debates, and was quite focused and competitive. He spent two years at the University of Queens, before taking a transfer to the University of Pennsylvania on a scholarship. Getting into an Ivy League college was a big deal, and he knew it would open more doors to bigger and better opportunities. He saw it as a chance to pursue a dual degree, so he enrolled himself in the Wharton School for a bachelor's degree in economics along with a degree in Physics.

At the University of Pennsylvania, he thrived in the physics department. He felt like more people accepted him there, and felt even more comfortable with the fellow physics students. He thought they were more like him and enjoyed lunches with them where they would discuss physics. At this time, he was in a long-distance relationship with his future wife Justine who stayed in Queens.

He made a close friend at Penn called Adeo Ressi, with whom he still shares a solid bond. He is now a Silicon Valley entrepreneur who created an empire of his own. He was a transfer student just like Elon and was placed in the same freshman dorm. Both of them disliked the social scene of the dorm and Adeo convinced Elon to rent a large off-campus house. They got a 10-bedroom house for a lower rate as it was supposed to be an unrented frat house. Both of them would focus on studies the entire week and then metamorphose the huge house into a nightclub. They would make it pitch dark using trash bags, and decorate the house to give it more of party atmosphere. Off campus, parties were still a rage in colleges, and almost 500 people would attend their parties every weekend. This would make them a few bucks because they would charge everyone 5 dollars for an 'all you can drink' party. But Elon never drank, and never did much at the parties. He would usually spend the party nights upstairs in his room, playing video games.

As time went by at UPenn, his interest in renewable sources of energy, especially solar energy, escalated, and he tried to explore new ways to harness it. Musk believed that three things would change the world and affect the future of humanity: sustainable energy like solar and wind power, the Internet, and life in space. He realized that it was important to figure out new technologies that would make solar cells more efficient. He wrote a paper on this exact topic, titled "The Importance of Being Solar", which accentuated the illustriousness of solar power technology and the improvements that are necessary to increase its potency.

He wrote a few more papers, one about compiling books, research documents, and articles into a single database by electronically scanning them just like an online library that could be easily accessed by everyone who wishes to write research papers. Another paper was a forty-page document about ultra-capacitors that Musk found rather fascinating. Capacitors are used to store electrical energy and his ideas about using them for space travel, cars, and aircraft were thought provoking and engaging. His professors gave excellent comments about his papers because of Musk's clarity concerning scientific phenomena and theories, as well as his compendious writing. He would explain complicated physics concepts with such ease and logic and inculcate that into his business plans. He knew he wanted to do something in the field of science, and look for profit on that path.

His father was an engineer, and Musk also considered himself to be an engineer and an inventor, more so than simply an entrepreneur. Musk began to think of his future more seriously and even contemplated about getting into the video game business. However, he decided against it because in his mind, video games wouldn't have the impact on the world he was striving for.

When he went for an interview, he would often make sure that the companies knew he had colossal and meaningful ideas that he would want to work on. He was aware that he would pursue the three fields that he always thought were credible, and they would undergo a large transformation in the near future.

In 1995, Musk applied and got accepted into Stanford University for a high-energy physics postgraduate program. But after two days of attending, he decided that it wasn't for him and dropped out to pursue an entrepreneurial career. He had a strong idea for a company, and he figured he didn't want to wait to get a post-graduate degree which wouldn't really benefit him.

Chapter 4: All Investments

Tesla Motors and SpaceX aren't the only companies in which Musk has invested, though they are possibly his most well known ventures. SpaceX has helped in bringing about a lot of change in the area of space exploration. Tesla Motors, his other company has helped in changing the trend of the automobile industry, and it has set a record by receiving thousands of pre-orders to the value of roughly $14-billion for their Tesla Model 3 car. As of October 2017, Musk's net worth is estimated at just under $20-billion. Musk is responsible for founding, investing in, and supporting multiple ventures. Here is a list of companies that he has invested in:

Zip2 Corporation

Zip2 was his first company, and it was the first online directory for the web. It was incorporated in the year 1995. Musk dropped out from the Ph.D. program in Physics at Stanford University in order to launch this company. Musk was 24 at the time. This online business helped in creating maps and online directories for newspapers. He managed to do this by linking up the maps available on Navteq to a business directory, and thereby successfully created the first online directory. After four years, he sold this company off for a good profit.

X.com

In the same year he sold Zip2, Musk incorporated an online payment company and named it X.com. He funded this from the sale proceeds of his previous company. This company focused on the development of technology that would enable online payments. Musk merged this company with his competitor, Confinity, and together they became PayPal. There was frequent ego, and personality clashes between the major stakeholders and this lead to the co-founders of Confinity to replacing Musk as the CEO of the company. This company was later on acquired by eBay.

Everdream Corporation

Musk invested in an IT company named Everdream Corporation in the year 1998. This company was eventually procured by Dell. In the year 1988, this company was cofounded by Lyndon Rive, Musk's cousin. Everdream Corporation dealt in providing desktop management services for businesses. Not just that, it also undertook the management of antivirus software, the performance of data backups, and the encryption of data. Musk was involved with PayPal at this time, and according to Silicon Valley Business Journal, Musk invested in this company during the fourth round. In the year 2007, Rive and his brother Russ sold this company to Dell.

SpaceX

Musk has always been fascinated by the concept of space exploration. This dream of his was fulfilled when he started SpaceX. This was a company based out in California that would manufacture rockets at an affordable price. This was a huge step in Musk's life and the launching of Falcon 9; their first rocket, was a dream come true. The first spacecraft that was manufactured by them was the Dragon, and this became the first ever commercial spacecraft that was used for transporting cargo between the ISS and Earth in the year 2012.

Musk Foundation

The Musk brothers started the Musk Foundation with the aim of providing grants for supporting research regarding renewable energy, space exploration, education in the field of science, engineering, diseases, and disorders. This Foundation has made a donation of around $785,000, and this includes a donation of $250,000 towards building the infrastructure for a city called Soma to be powered by solar energy in Japan, after a tsunami destroyed most of it in 2011.

Tesla Motors

As previously mentioned, Musk invested a lot in Tesla Motors in their opening round of investment in 2003. Musk then joined this company as a member of its board of directors. The first car of Tesla was the Roadster, and it managed to pleasantly surprise all the customers with the sports car like features and the fact that it was capable of accelerating from 0 to 60 miles per hour in less than four seconds. After the market collapsed in the year 2008, Musk started to take quite an active role in the working of the company, and took over the role of CEO. The Model S of Tesla was a highly successful car which managed to create quite a buzz in the market.

Surrey Satellite Technology

In the year 2005, Musk acquired a small stake of about 10% in a small satellite provider. He was of the notion that this would provide SpaceX with an opportunity for thinking about becoming the most successful vendor of small as well as inexpensive spacecraft in the world. This would help in creating business opportunities for his company, SpaceX. Surrey Satellite Technology is responsible for building radio satellites; it also deals with the launching and operation of small spacecrafts with the purpose of monitoring the weather, communications, and varied other purposes.

SolarCity

Musk has always been interested in the field of sustainable energy and the development green technology. Keeping in tune with the energy saving proponents of Tesla, he invested heavily in SolarCity. This is one of the largest installers of solar panels for domestic purposes in the USA. This company was founded by Lyndon and Peter Rive, his cousins, in the year 2006. He is now the CEO of this company as well. SolarCity works towards developing designs and the installation of solar energy systems for providing clean energy. It also performs the function of auditing and building electric vehicle charging stations. In the year 2005, SolarCity made an announcement of partnering with Tesla for incorporating the batteries designed by the latter in their solar-battery system.

Mahalo.com

When Mahalo was launched in the year 2007, Musk invested. This website is akin to Wikipedia, Quora, Ask Jeeves, and the like. However, it incorporates the features of all the three mentioned sites in one. This site allows the users to post and answer questions posted by the other users. When Google overhauled the search function of this company, it was forced to lay off around 10% of their staff in the year 2011. It has then changed its company strategy towards creating original how-to-videos, plus a live user-generated question and answer session.

Stripe

Once Musk was no longer a part of PayPal, he chose to invest in one of its rivals. This company was Stripe, and its main goal is to allow different online applications as well as businesses such as Lyft and Facebook to accept payments from virtually anywhere in the world. This company was recently valued at roughly $5-billion, and it has also recently entered a new partnership with Twitter.

Halcyon Molecular Inc

In the year 2008, this ambitious and futuristic biotechnology startup was incorporated by William Andregg and his brother Michael Andregg. Their goal was to accommodate the secrets that are hidden within the DNA. According to Gigaom, this company, in 2009 had said that they wanted to sequence a pure human genome within ten minutes for less than $100. This company was competing with other companies that were working in the same field, and it had to ultimately shut its operations in the year 2012.

Tesla Science Center

In the year 2014, Musk made a donation of $1 million towards a new science museum that was dedicated to Nikola Tesla. Tesla was one of the greatest inventors in history. This science center is located in Wardenclyffe, in the city of New York. This was built in the exact location where Nikola Tesla built a giant transmitter tower for experimenting with sending messages as well as shuttling about wireless electricity. Musk has plans for developing a Tesla supercharge station in the parking lot of this center. This charging station is planned to be the quickest one in the world.

Chapter 5: Zip2 and PayPal

Perhaps the second greatest decision that Elon Musk took was in the summer of 1995. Some consider this to be the most important decision of his life. He wanted to pursue a Ph.D. in Applied Physics and had enrolled himself at the well-known Stanford University. Within two days of joining the University, he left his pursuit of academics and started his first company. It was an IT company named Zip2. Musk started this with his brother Kimbal.

The office of this company was located in a warehouse, and Musk used to not only work long hours there, but also live there. Whenever he needed to shower, he would go to one of the locker rooms in the stadium. This helped him to save up sufficient money to keep his company afloat during the initial years.

The internet started growing in popularity around the same time. At this time though, not many believed that they could make a fortune out the web. However, Musk was amongst the first ones to believe otherwise. In the year 1999, Elon Musk sold his company Zip2 for $307 million in cash, and about $34 million in securities. He sold Zip2 to AltaVista, the biggest search engine of that time and it was later on acquired by Compaq. This seal was the biggest deal that was recorded for selling a company for cash. Musk used a portion of these earnings to buy himself a house that he renovated completely, as well as a McLaren F1.

In the same year, Musk began working on a system for electronic payments. This was where the future was headed, and he knew it. He started X.com, and this became his new business venture. In the year 2000, Musk decided to merge his company with that of his rival, Confinity. Confinity was owned by Max Levchin and Peter Thiel. Confinity was a software company. This company provided software that would let people who used

Palm Pilots and PDAs to store all their bank details in an encrypted format. It was in the year 2001 that X.com was rechristened as PayPal. Musk became the CEO as well as the Chairman of PayPal.

There were quite a few disagreements that cropped up amongst the heads of the company since they all had quite differing ideas. However, all these disagreements never affected the company dynamics or the growth of the company. The models that Musk had started to develop for his business led to successful marketing. This, in turn, led to the rapid growth in the number of customers.

It was in the year 2002 that eBay acquired PayPal. The deal was finalized at $1.5 billion, and Musk received $180 million from the sale proceeds. Musk made use of this for funding his other interests. These interests included finding alternative sources of energy and space engineering. This is where his journey in the field of internet businesses ended.

Chapter 6: Space Exploration Technologies

Elon Musk has always followed the first principle of thought. He actually believes that people should try to understand the cause of a problem for obtaining the final solution. Here is an example of how Musk made use of this line of thinking in his businesses. During an interview, he had said that people all over the world would find that battery packs are quite expensive. This is because of the simple fact that they had been expensive in the past as well. They would probably say that "it costs about $300 per watt-hour and it is never going to go down". Well, this is where everyone tends to go wrong.

If you make use of the first principles of thinking, then you would have probably thought differently. Musk says that by asking the right questions, you will certainly be able to identify the actual cost of anything. Here are a few possible questions that you could ask. "What materials would be used in a battery?" and "what is the cost of these components in the market?"

The materials that are used in a battery are nickel, carbon, aluminum, steel, and a polymer that is used for separation. You will simply need to identify the price at which these basic materials are being offered. If you manage to find the actual price of these components, then you will deduce that the battery packs would only cost about $50 per watt-hour. Now, you will need to come up with a way in which you can make use of these elements and then combine all of this into a battery cell. You will realize that it is cheaper than what you would have originally thought. This is precisely how Musk managed to start his company SpaceX that would allow him to pursue his dream of space engineering.

It was in the year 2001 that Musk decided it was about time that humans try and colonize Mars! He came up with the concept of

Mars Oasis. The idea of this project was to send a greenhouse with a few crops so that they could be grown in the soil of Mars. The main aim of this project was to promote public interest in the field of space exploration. In the same year, Musk traveled to Moscow along with Adeo Ressi and Jim Cantrell to purchase refurbished ICBMs. These would enable them to send payloads to the International Space Station as was envisioned by NASA and other aerospace engineering organizations.

The trio met with a lot of companies. However, most of these companies believed that Musk was a novice and that his ideas shouldn't be taken too seriously. So, they returned to the United States without any progress. In 2002, during February the trio returned to Russia to look for ICBMs once again. However, this time they had taken Mike Griffin along with them. Mike Griffin was in the CIA and had also previously worked at NASA. He was given a bid of $8-million for buying a rocket. Musk had decided that this was quite expensive and had decided that he was better off starting a new company of his own where he could build rockets that were affordable.

Like mentioned above, Musk discovered that he could procure the necessary raw materials at a fraction of the market value of the commodity and then build his own rocket! He also identified that by vertical integration, his company (SpaceX) would not only be able to cut costs by ten times, but it would also be able to enjoy a huge profit margin of 70%. This was when Musk made up his mind about starting SpaceX.

Musk realized that he could build his own rockets instead of buying really expensive ones from others. He started out by reaching out to other innovators and technicians who were a part of the aerospace industry in America. He managed to rope in a few seasoned engineers as well as technical specialists away from their jobs in big companies, and got them to join SpaceX. They began working for him in the headquarters of SpaceX located in California. However, attracting venture capital was a completely different ballgame altogether. Well, to be fair, space isn't exactly within the comfort zone of a venture capitalist. Since he couldn't attract the necessary investment from external sources, Musk ultimately had to invest his own money for this project. The risk he took paid off, and his company was amongst the first ones to manufacture the first reusable rocket within the private sector.

Musk has made use of $100 million of his fortune in setting up SpaceX. He is the CEO as well as the CTO of this company. Musk has worked on projects for developing as well as manufacturing launch vehicles for space, with the intention of expanding and extending the knowledge of rocket technology. Falcon1 and Falcon 9 rockets are the first two launch vehicles that were manufactured by SpaceX.

The first spacecraft designed and manufactured by them was Dragon. These launch vehicles, as well as the spacecraft, were manufactured within the first seven years of the incorporation of this company. The proudest moment for SpaceX was when the rocket, Falcon1, was the first privately funded launch vehicle to satellite the Earth's orbit. It was in the year 2012 that SpaceX reached its peak. This was when the Dragon was berthed with the International Space Station. SpaceX had successfully become the first commercial company to launch its own spacecraft and have its berth at the ISS.

Musk and his team got to work immediately. They started working on developing two kinds of Falcon rockets. The name for these rockets was inspired by Star Wars. In the movies, the spacecraft was called as "Millennium Falcon". Their aim was to develop a rocket by making use of existing technology; at the lowest cost they possibly could manage. For instance, Falcon 1 makes use of a pintle engine that can be traced back to the 60s. It has got a single fuel injector. Whereas the rockets that are usually used by NASA (National Aeronautics and Space Administration) have a showerhead design that has got multiple fuel injectors in it. SpaceX also needed theodolite that is made use of for aligning rockets.

Instead of having to buy a new one, they managed to save $25,000 by purchasing one on the Internet site, eBay. There are other expensive costs that need to be incurred when it comes to designing and manufacturing rockets. The design that Musk opted for was a reusable rocket. This meant that the company would need to acquire the first stage of the rocket, which it sheds when leaving the Earth's atmosphere.

In 2006, SpaceX received a contract from NASA. This was also a difficult period for Musk has he had run out of funds. He was trying to borrow from a lot of people, and was waiting on NASA to tell him the result of their deal. It was only when NASA accepted his tender that he was able to rise to his original status. The contract was written so that he could continue the development of the rocket (Falcon 9) and for making use of the spacecraft (Dragon) for transporting any cargo to the International Space Station (ISS). NASA and Musk entered into a contract that would require him to launch Falcon 9 into space, and the Dragon would be launched 12 times for carrying any cargo into space. This would be the replacement of the US Space Shuttle once it would be retired from operations in the year 2011. The company Soyuz was the only way in which astronauts could be shuttled to the ISS. However, in the year 2014, SpaceX was also recognized as one of the companies that would work towards identifying a route for transporting astronauts to ISS in a simpler manner.

At present, SpaceX is considered to be the largest producer of rocket motors. Not just that, but it also holds the record of having motors which have the highest thrust to weight ratio. Calculations show that SpaceX has produced more than 100 Merlin 1D engines that are not only operational but also are superior motors. The power of the Merlin 1D motor is such that it would be able to hold the weight of 40 family cars at one go!

The combination of Merlin 1D motor and the Falcon rockets is the best combination currently out there.

Elon Musk has always been a voracious reader and was deeply influenced by the book "The Foundation Series" written by Isaac Asimov. The views about space exploration that were mentioned in that book appealed to him, and he started believing in them. Musk believes that for the continuation of the human race, it would be better to start looking for alternative ways in which life could be continued on other planets. There is a possibility that human beings might also face extinction as dinosaurs did. The likelihood of being hit by an asteroid or even the eruption of a volcano is possible. The possibility of a widespread epidemic or even being sucked into a black hole shouldn't be ignored. Musk had once stated that he would like it if human beings could colonize Mars. That would be something, wouldn't it? Well, Elon Musk is full of surprises.

Chapter 7: Tesla Motors

After eBay acquired PayPal for $1.5 billion, Elon was offered $180 million for the deal. With this money, he invested $100 million is SpaceX, $70 million in Tesla and $10 million in Solar City. He knew from the beginning that he wanted to make progress in three specific fields - the Internet, renewable energy and space exploration.

Musk was very much into the prospect of using electricity to run cars, and he became a major investor of Tesla in 2004, helping to get it started. The business plan consisted of primarily three steps. Firstly, to create a sports car which would be premium and high-performance and compete with the other cars in the market. Secondly, introduce a luxury vehicle that could be capable of giving a tough fight to extravagant brands like Mercedes and BMW. Thirdly, to mass-produce reasonably priced electric vehicles for the common people. Tesla was founded by Marc Tarpenning and Martin Eberhard and is committed to manufacturing affordable electric cars. In 2006, Tesla introduced their first electric car, The Tesla Roadster that was a sports model. It was an economical and affordable two-seater car. This car could go from 0 to 97 km per hour in about 4 seconds. It was their way of showing that electric cars could be just as good and efficient as the ones that run on gas.

After this initial step in which the Roadster sold just a little more than 1300 units, it was time to start the ground work for the implementation of the second step. In 2009, the government allotted a loan of $465-million as funding to put phase two into action, which was manufacturing a four-door sedan that would challenge the car industry and the big names. The only problem was that Musk didn't have a manufacturing unit and Tesla was outsourcing majority of the parts required for the Roadster and then assembling them in a garage behind their showroom in Menlo Park, California. Mass production of the parts required for the new Tesla Model S was not possible. Musk figured he needed an area that was big enough like the one he had seen in Nummi, which was the plant for the production of Toyota cars. He also knew that the property was valued at nearly $1 billion, which was way out of budget for a startup.

But fortunately for Musk, the tour invitation for the Nummi plant that was extended to him by Akio Toyota was for a serious reason. Akio was trying to pique Musk's interest in buying the plant and wanted to keep it under the covers so that it wouldn't attract the attention of the media. This was because the automobile industry was in a state of depression after the economic recession in 2008. The General Manager of the Nummi plant had already declared bankruptcy and retreated in 2009, leaving Toyota to put their products to halt in less than a month. This meant that the 200-acre car factory was up for grabs and hence Toyoda created an opportunity for Musk.

Musk found his golden ticket, it was all that he needed, and he made an offer of $42 million for the factory. He heard back a month later and was rather surprised to know that his offer had been accepted. He thought he had offered a low amount for a factory of that size and stature, but when he visited the second time as the owner of the plant, he saw the repairs that would be needed to get the plant back on track and working. He knew it was going to be a very laborious undertaking. Tesla had just completed an initial public offer and had more that $700 million at their disposal that was to be used for modifying the factory to their needs.

In retrospect, circa 2006, Tesla was in a financial crisis over the production of the Roadster. It was estimated that the delivery of the car would be sometime in 2007 and profits would start coming in around 2008, but an audit suggested that the car would cost more than Tesla estimated and something had to be done about it. Structural changes in the car were necessary so that it could adhere to the technical specifications.

Complications started increasing, and more funds were put into the production of the Roadster, and the schedule of production was disrupted.

Tesla had to bring in a new CEO, so Eberhard could concentrate on the next product, which was the Model S sedan. While stress regarding the shape, structure, and materials used to build the vehicle was at an all time high, tensions started to ensue between the Musk and Eberhard. The search for a new CEO had begun, and Musk did not find any candidate worthy of the position. After a board meeting which excluded Eberhard, the board voted that it was best to let Eberhard go as he was not proving beneficial to the company anymore, but he remained a shareholder. From there, Musk took over as the CEO.

As 2012 dawned, Tesla halted the production of the Roadster to focus on the new Model S sedan, which received a lot of praise from the automotive critics for its layout and operations. It had more efficient batteries, which were underneath the car, giving it added storage space. With the new plant on the cards, Tesla had more on its plate than it imagined. They had to hire a workforce, make nice with the worker's unions and compete in a market that had big names like General Motors and Nissan. But, with Musk's determination as Tesla's financial standing turned around, he managed to set up the plant without facing too many complications.

Musk managed to roll out the Model S, which was the company's first electric sedan. It was honored as The Car of the Year in 2013 by Motor Trend magazine. After this grand success, in late 2014 Musk unraveled two dual motor versions of Model S, which were improved for better performance, handling, and efficiency. Tesla launched their Model X SUV in 2015.

Musk oversees the entire functioning of the company right from the designing, engineering, finances, product development, marketing, and research. Tesla has revolutionized the outlook of the world towards using sustainable and clean energy to power a vehicle. It has brought about tremendous development in the technology used in electric cars, solar components, and battery products.

Tesla has managed to make quite a name for itself, and with Musk as its CEO, Tesla is destined to reach great heights.

Chapter 8: SolarCity

In the year 2006, Musk co-founded SolarCity. This is a company that would provide photovoltaic products and allied services. He started this company along with his cousin Lyndon Rive. Solar City is the provider of various energy services and has its headquarters in the city of San Mateo, California. The company has a workforce of over 13,000 employees, and it specializes in the designing, financing, marketing, as well as the installation of power systems that are solar powered. This company has managed to grow at a rapid pace and has been extremely helpful in the installation of solar powered photovoltaic systems in America.

SolarCity has indeed played quite an important part in improving the statistics when it comes to the installation of solar panels in the country. Lyndon and Peter Rive came up with the idea of starting and launching this company based on the suggestions of their cousin, Elon Musk. He not only helped them with the development of this idea, but he had also helped them in setting it up. Later on, Musk was appointed as the Chairman of SolarCity.

Within a period of one year of its establishment, this company managed to become the biggest supplier of solar energy for domestic purposes in California. Like mentioned earlier, the headquarters of this company is located in San Mateo. However, its operations are carried on via several distribution centers that are located all over the US. These centers are the service providers for the particular locality and would help in providing energy to that area.

SolarCity has been able to specialize in the marketing as well as designing of numerous products. This company initially started off with the idea of providing solar energy; and they quickly introduced the concept of solar leasing for homeowners. This would help all the homeowners who have installed this technology to save substantially on their energy bills.

In the year 2008, the company completed two huge solar installations on a commercial scale in San Jose and San Francisco. They have also installed solar equipment for commercial purposes for big names like British Motor Car Distributors, Walmart, Intel, and even for the U.S. Army. In the year 2009, SolarCity acquired a company named SolSource. SolSource is an energy business that has also diversified into the manufacturing of various electric chargers that can be made use of for charging the batteries of vehicles.

In the year 2011, SolarCity had announced that they were launching a huge project, named Solar Strong. The aim of this project would be the provision of energy to the privatized homes of various military personnel.

In the year 2013, SolarCity took over the operation of Zep Solar through an acquisition. This helped them in venturing into the development of solar panels that are capable of being mounted on top of the roofs.

Right after this company was launched, it managed to start providing solar energy to the residential units situated in California and within a period of one year, it had grown to become the largest supplier of the same area. The Solar Power World Magazine named SolarCity as the second best Solar Installation Company in the US in the year 2013.

Chapter 9: Neuralink and OpenAI

Neuralink

In the year 2016, Elon Musk founded Neuralink. This neurotechnological startup has undertaken the mission of integrating the human mind with AI (Artificial Intelligence). The main aim is to create devices that are capable of being implanted into the human brain and will help the human mind merge with software. Musk is the CEO of Neuralink, Tesla, and SpaceX. Neuralink wants to turn the cloud-based AI into a mere extension of the human mind. The company is working on a product that will help those who have suffered brain injuries.

Neuralink is hoping to get such a device out into the market with the next couple of years. Musk hopes that this will help human beings to communicate via consensual therapy. Neuralink is perhaps the first time that Elon Musk has shown a keen interest in the merging of human beings with machines. At the launch of Tesla in Dubai, Musk had said something about the need for human beings to transform themselves into cyborgs if they want to be able to stand a chance against the rise of artificial intelligence. He hopes to be able to merge biological and digital intelligence. This is referred to as Transhumanism, and this would result in a great enhancement of the capabilities of human beings by making use of science and technology. In his own way, Musk is also working towards the same concept. Just like he did with all his other business ventures, even with Neuralink, he is taking up one realistic challenge at a time.

OpenAI

In the year 2015, in the month of December, Musk announced the creation of OpenAI. This is a research company that works towards the development of artificial intelligence for helping out humanity. Musk is the cofounder as well as the chairman of OpenAI. This is a non-profit research company and works on developing AI that is safe, and also ensuring that the distribution of AI is done as evenly as possible. There are about 60 full-time researchers and engineers employed by OpenAI. The company's focus is on long-term research, and working on problems that would require certain advancement in the capabilities of AI. The information that they have discovered is often posted on the blogs maintained by them.

Chapter 10: Philosophies

Elon Musk is quite dynamic and driven. He believes in his ideas and he knows that he can make a difference in this world. Behind all this, there are a few philosophies that he believes in.

Personal Philosophy

In one of the commencement speeches that Musk has given, he said that there was a time when he faced an existential crisis. He was trying to figure out what everything meant, their purpose, and his own purpose. He has always believed that human beings are capable of extending their consciousness by simply asking the right questions. This happens to be the only way in which they can be enlightened and the only way for the entire human race to move forward.

The philosophy behind Musk's thinking is quite complex and exciting at the same time. His thinking and philosophies revolve around the word 'consciousness'. There are some cases when Musk has made a reference to the light that constitutes consciousness. Musk has always believed that human beings have got a precious quality that is unique and it is their consciousness. This is a unique quality, and he believes that this should be nurtured. However, he never actually explained why he considers knowledge to be unique or precious. The gaps in this theory can be understood better with the help of the works of Sagan. Sagan was of the opinion that human beings are solely responsible for the expansion of the universe. People are constantly trying to not just understand themselves, but are also trying to become aware of their purpose on this earth.

If you assume that Musk had the same inclination towards cosmology as Sagan, you will understand why he believes that the key to identify or understand oneself lies with expanding one's consciousness. There are a lot of things in the universe that are valuable. But, a unique character that humanity possesses is that we can think and also develop a sense of self awareness, which helps us to obtain more information about the universe and ourselves. It would be wrong to assume that animals have neither of the two traits that are considered valuable. But, the truth is that these traits are not as developed in them as they are developed in humans.

Human beings have a very high sense of self, but we do not understand the universe or ourselves the way we should. Luckily, human beings have the capacity to expand the knowledge that they possess. This leaves us in a position that is both unique and privileged. It has been noticed that the universe has seemed both silent and daft. But, human beings have the power to wake the universe up! The universe has been hibernating for the last million years. Musk appears to see it as his responsibility to wake it up!

Musk, being an engineer, scientist, and a philosopher to an extent has realized that human beings have been restricted by their physical self when it comes to learning more. The easiest and the most accurate way by which we can extend our knowledge with our physical restrictions is exploration through technology, and the way in which we utilize that technology. There is a possibility that all human being would be unable to arrive at all the answers. But, when they are willing to learn, they would reach out further towards sources that will help them learn more and ask more questions. The truth is that not every person on this planet desires to know. There are only a few people who have the urge to know more. These people have a temperament of the highest order. This is what makes Musk a great philosopher at heart.

This philosophy distinguishes Musk from the rest. He an imagination that most men do not possess. He has an imagination that has expanded more than it has for most humans. He has allowed his thoughts to soar to places where most of us would not have dared. He has all the resources that he needs to back his thoughts up – the resources, intelligence and the initiative to make the thoughts come true!

His Business Philosophy

At a point in time, Musk decided that he wanted to become a physicist and applied to Stanford University in pursuit of that goal. However, he decided to discontinue this when a lasting impression had been made on him. The most important learning experience was when he understood the first principles of thinking. This technique of thinking revolves around identifying the root of a problem for obtaining a solution. He believes that he would be able to attain a better answer for any problem by applying the first principles of thinking instead of regular analogy. He believes that most human beings tend to go about their lives by reasoning through analogy. When people do that, they are following the routine that every other person has been following. When you follow the first principles, you are letting yourself understand the truth! You are letting yourself understand the fundamentals and then reason with yourself from there.

This method of thinking isn't new and has been around for centuries now. Aristotle, over 2000 years ago, said that the best way to pursue any goal is to attack it from the first principles. Musk has admitted that he uses a lot of his mental energy when it comes to using the first principles. He also believes that he ends up with results that are earth shattering and novel! The first principle was what he used when he was looking at starting one of his companies called SpaceX.

When Musk had to get a rough estimate of the funds that they would require for building their rocket, they didn't settle for the information that was available on the Internet. They had broken down the process of building a rocket into different parts and then figured out the cost that they would have to incur for building each of these parts. At the end of all their research, they had managed to come to a conclusion that they could build a rocket at a tiny fraction of the cost of what was available on the market.

Chapter 11: Overcoming Obstacles

Everyone has to face obstacles, and it is quite natural. Even Musk had to face certain challenges and even failures at times. However, he did not let any of these so-called failures or obstacles deter him from achieving the goals he had set for himself. Before achieving the success that he has, he had to go through quite a rough patch.

Musk was a typical nerd while growing up and was always busy reading something or tinkering with computers. He was never good at socializing and wasn't a social being. He was quite awkward and was certainly weaker when compared to the other students in his school. This made him an extremely easy target for all the bullies at school. He was beaten up quite a few times, and after an extremely horrible incident, he was hospitalized. Even today, he has trouble breathing due to the injury that he sustained. However, this didn't deter him

Not many are aware of this, but Musk once applied for a job at Netscape. However, he never received any reply from them due to his lack of a science background. He had degrees in both economics as well as physics. He had even gone to their office to talk to them but returned empty handed since he was too shy to talk to anyone. This was when he decided that he would simply pursue his own ideas and would set up his own business. He started Zip2 after this. This might not seem like a big deal that he wasn't given a job at Netscape, but it should be taken into consideration that this was one of the leading companies in technology at that point in time.

Musk and his brother founded Zip2. However, the board of directors of this company ousted Musk at its CEO, claiming that they were thinking about the welfare of the company in the long run. The board made a claim that he couldn't be the CEO of the company since he didn't have any required operational responsibilities. His inexperience was also one of the reasons quoted to him. Musk had been the founder of X.com, and this was later on transformed into PayPal in 2000. Musk had been declared as the CEO of the new company. He had gotten into an argument with the CTO of the company at that time about wanting to go ahead with Windows. This disagreement led to him being ousted as the CEO of PayPal while he was on vacation!

While he had gone on a vacation to South Africa, his native country, he had a near death experience. He was attacked by a severe case of cerebral malaria that has a mortality rate of 20%, even after being treated. It took him about six months to fully recover from the disease, and he lost around 40 lbs during this period. He always says that his close brush with death had given him renewed vigor and focus to keep going.

Musk suffered an incredible tragedy when his son died. Musk and his first wife, Justine Wilson conceived their first son, and they had named him Nevada Alexander. He was ten weeks old when he died of SIDS (Sudden Infant Death Syndrome). By the time the paramedics had reached the baby, the baby had died due to a deprivation of oxygen. Musk has never spoken about this incident in public.

Musk had come up with the idea of "Mars Oasis". However, when he went to Russia to procure the necessary ICBMs, the companies turned him down. He needed these ICBMs for transporting the necessary payloads into space. After he was turned down the first time, Musk decided to visit the companies in Russia once again. This time around, he was offered quite an expensive deal for acquiring the rockets he needed. However, this did not discourage him. In fact, this pushed him to think harder, and this was when he decided to launch SpaceX.

The money that he had received from the sale of PayPal was invested in SpaceX by Musk. The first three launches that were attempted by the company failed and they had sufficient funds for just one last attempt. The company was almost close to becoming bankrupt, and it was quite a testing time for everyone involved. However, the fourth launch proved to be quite successful, and this was when they received the contract from NASA for making use of the rockets and the spacecraft designed by SpaceX.

The first electric car unveiled by Tesla was the Roadster. This wasn't a cost efficient vehicle, and its launch was delayed considerably due to severe financial crunch. In fact, the company was in need of a desperate infusion of funds, and it was close to shutting its doors forever. This was when the financial crisis had hit the world and Musk had to make a risky decision to save the company. Musk had decided to invest all of his life savings into the company to save it, and it proved to be a good decision in the end.

The key takeaway from all this is that it doesn't matter if you don't achieve success immediately. If you believe in yourself, you can do it.

Conclusion

45

Thanks again for taking the time to read this book!

You should now have a good understanding of Elon Musk and his fascinating life!

If you enjoyed this book, please take the time to leave me a review on Amazon. I appreciate your honest feedback, and it really helps me to continue producing high quality books.